All Scripture references taken from KJV unless otherwise indicated.

**EVIL TOUCH** by Dr. Marlene Miles

Freshwater Press

ISBN: 978-1-960150-48-6

Paperback Version

Copyright 2023 by Dr. Marlene Miles

All rights reserved.

All rights reserved. No part of this book may be reproduced, distributed, or transmitted by any means or in any means including photocopying, recording or other electronic or mechanical methods without prior written permission of the publisher except in the case of brief publications or critical reviews.

## Table of Contents

Shopping .................................................................... 4
A Visitation ................................................................ 8
Now Leaving the State ............................................. 15
*Love*, In the Time of COVID .................................... 18
Not In the Physical ................................................... 21
What Did You Dream? ............................................. 26
The Touch of God ..................................................... 29
Evil Handwriting ....................................................... 30
Evil Hands ................................................................. 35
You Are *Not* in Good Hands .................................. 38
Can We Pray Yet? ..................................................... 41
It Don't Feel *Too Good* .......................................... 47
Redemption & Reversal ........................................... 48
Let's Pray .................................................................. 54
You're Pulling My Leg ............................................... 60
The Womb ................................................................ 75
Root Cause, Not Just Symptoms .............................. 79
Deliver Me from Wicked Hands ............................... 91
Strange Hands .......................................................... 95
Can't Touch This ....................................................... 99
Prayerbooks by this author .................................... 108
Other books by this author .................................... 109

# Evil Touch

Freshwater Press USA

# Shopping

It was around 2:00 or 2:30 in the afternoon; I was out shopping. *Man--*, COVID really changed things, I couldn't believe I was really out and about. I was in a department store, that reminded me of the Macy's on 34<sup>th</sup> Street, but drabber, standing on a platform of some sort, with my back to the main store aisle, spinning a counter display that held either earrings or broaches, I'm not sure. Nothing caught my attention as I really do not like shopping. So, it would have been unlike me to linger at this counter or spend too much time spinning the bijoux carousel.

I wondered as it spun why I was standing at the countertop and not looking *in* a case with a salesperson--- *at my age*. Costume jewelry is usually on display and I'm not in the market for costume jewelry that much, anymore. There is nothing new under the sun, and I've worn all that stuff before. It's been in and out of style at least once, maybe twice since my mother gave me permission to wear earrings in my late teens. So, I'm content with jewelry I have and usually just recycle that.

Abruptly, I felt a touch on my left elbow. Interesting, even though I was wearing a coat or some garment with long sleeves I felt that **touch** on my elbow—not the *sleeve* of the jacket or coat, but on my actual elbow.

I turned about and standing there in the department store aisle was a woman who appeared to also be a shopper, not a salesperson. She was shorter than I am. Of course, I was on a platform, but she was definitely shorter. She looked intently at me. I looked at her, knowing that I didn't know her. It was a soft staring standoff. I don't think either of us won, but I didn't blink. As she was getting a look at me, I was getting a look at her.

She was drab in appearance, dull. It wasn't her complexion that made her look dull, but it's that she had no light about her. She had a shorter pixie-like haircut that was also lackluster. She wore a buttoned up black coat that was belted closed. It seemed to be made of wool or some heavy, wintry fabric.

Now, I'm one to find something great about everyone I meet or see, something different, unique, even lovely. And I usually give compliments easily. But there was absolutely nothing special about her. There were no lights about her, there was no glow. There really wasn't any *life* about her. She didn't speak; there was no smile. She just looked at me. She could almost have been a cardboard cutout, really.

I looked back at her. If you are so rude as to stare and not speak, then *we won't* be *speaking*.

I still could feel that touch where she touched my left elbow.

There was no emotion. No fear. No excitement. No nothing. More like a staring contest and for what purpose had to be discovered.

I woke up from my afternoon nap; I had been dreaming--, about shopping. Still, I began to try to figure this *dream* out. I had my opinions as to who she was, after all *who would need to have a good look at me*? I decided she was the *deceased* wife of the man I was dating.

This wasn't just a dream, else, how could I still *feel* the touch? It didn't burn or tingle, it just felt like a touch. But why? I thought the touch was to get my attention, because it wasn't until she touched me that I turned around and faced her. I thought she was mistaking me for someone else. That has happened more than once in my life and twice it happened in a shopping mall. Three times if you count this *dream,* **if** it really was mistaken identity.

# A Visitation

A *visitation* is a supernatural occurrence, it is expected and well-received and called a divine visitation when the Lord visits, when the Holy Spirit overshadows and "visits," or when the Angel of the Lord, or the Angel of the Lord's presence visits, such as when Jacob wrestled with the Angel of God.

Visitations are divine when God is behind it and bringing glory, blessings, prophecy and purpose into the Earth. As long as we are moving according to our destiny clock, we should **expect** divine visitation from the Lord, at times.

Had that been a dream or a *visitation*? If this was really a *visitation--,* how cool is this? Like any **ignorant** person I felt this was a good thing. This dream, to me, meant that *I'm spiritual*.

If the deceased wife of a man that I'm dating is coming to check me out, then maybe this man is serious about me and praying to GOD about me. This made sense to me because I'm saved; it would be appropriate for him to ask God about me. Maybe he's talking to his dead wife--. She's *dead* but she's interested in the well-being of her former Earth spouse and is checking me out to make sure he's okay.

**I mentioned that I was ignorant, right?**

**IGGG-NORR-RRANT!!!**

So, I called my most spiritual friend, told her all about it, and she confirmed that this was a *visitation*. I've not known her to be ignorant, but she told me that you don't tell anyone about a *visitation*. I really wanted to tell him, but she told me, "*Don't*."

I believed my friend's counsel for two days.

Then I told it to my second most spiritual friend. We *ooh'ed* and *ahh'ed* and marveled at the fact that I could still *feel* the touch. And whatever could it mean?

The third person I told mused together with me, but we were troubled as to how a deceased person could get permission from God to do what no other deceased person can do – come and *visit* someone who is *alive*?

A rich man in Hades saw Lazarus in the arms of Abraham and pleaded for a drop of water. The answer was, *No*. Then the dead rich man asked if someone could go back from the dead and warn his family that hell and the devil really exist. That answer was also, *No*. So how can a **dead** woman come to take a look at a *living* woman who is dating the man that she used to be married to in her Earth life? Nope. Not happening.

> He answered, 'Then I beg you, father, send Lazarus to my family, for I have five brothers. Let him warn them, so that they will not also come to this place of torment.
>
> Abraham replied, 'They have Moses and the Prophets; let them listen to them.
>
> No, father Abraham,' he said, 'but if someone from the dead goes to them, they will repent.

> He said to him, 'If they do not listen to Moses and the Prophets, they will not be convinced even if someone rises from the dead.(Luke 16:27-31)

My whole ignorant theory was falling apart. Was this a *masquerade* because even dead the woman didn't look like herself, like, maybe she had deteriorated in the grave or something. (Remember, I'm ignorant then.)

If this was a divine visitation, what *angel* was she and why didn't she look **divine**? Or speak? Why didn't she look pretty, or happy? Why didn't she look shiny, glorious, or glowing? Why was there absolutely NO light around this person? And why was she wearing all that black? She didn't even look like any other pictures that I had previously seen of the dearly departed woman, Lord, rest her soul.

It was disappointing, actually, seeing an alleged dead person who has possibly has *permission* to return to look at *me*, shouldn't she have had some glory on her? There was no glory.

Ichabod. All Ichabod.

This troubled me for a few weeks. Then my inner P.I. came out and began to sleuth in earnest. I reviewed the pictures I had seen of the deceased woman, and it was NOT her. It absolutely was NOT the deceased wife. Of course, not--, like she came back to *shop*?

Soon I forgot about it.

Weeks later, not intending to discover anything in particular I saw a picture of a woman and THAT WAS HER, **that** was the woman from the department store "dream" which was really a *visitation*.

That was her!

It was not his deceased spouse, but it was an alive person that **he** knows. He has mentioned her and, well--, thank you, social media. There was no glory on her living picture either. Nothing. More Ichabod. This was NOT a *divine* visitation. There was nothing divine about it. No angelic choir, no sound to it, just silence. So, was she just being nosey, coming to look at me?

The plot didn't thicken just then, it congealed. It solidified.

Since I was now in the mode of telling anyone I wanted to tell about this *visitation* that my so-called *spiritual* friend had said should remain secret, I asked the only person this drab woman and myself had in common, my boyfriend, *What up with that?*

He didn't *know*. Or he feigned that he didn't know.

I really only had one question of him, *Why would his friend need to have a close look at me?* He shot some words at me like heavy cannon balls from a cartoon cannon, big ineffective ammo, and then he slowed down his rambling. I clearly remember the short sentence, *"Things change."* Oh he was beginning to come clean that they had a relationship. Then he stopped short of confessing anything and said he didn't know and became defensive and angry.

When I thought it was his departed wife, I had asked him if his Earth wife was small, but also had told him I thought I had seen her and why didn't she look pretty? I mean, where had her "pretty" gone?

One of us was now furious and it was not me. Is this why you don't tell people about *visitations*? Is it because they become angry?

I didn't mind. I don't mind telling people the truth, even if it is uncomfortable, inconvenient or causes anger.

The phone line went silent.

Ichabod.

And, even so, he was treating her horribly if they were a couple. I say that because I was getting mega attention from him. How dare he. A real woman doesn't want some one else's husband or *man*.

# Now Leaving the State

You've seen those signs on the Interstate that read, Now Leaving the State of _____ and when entering another: Welcome to _____. Yeah, that's how I felt as I left the State of **Ignorance**, and crossed over the state line, into the State of **Knowledge** as I learned what in tarnation happened to me in that department store *visitation*.

**It was an EVIL TOUCH.**

It was an **evil touch** by a witch, in the spirit. In person, if I can say that because she either didn't bother to disguise herself, or she failed at being hidden or disguised, **<u>BUT GOD</u>**. God showed me this thing, as she came to put her hands on me. Yes, I just called someone a witch. It was not mistaken identity, *I* was the target, and it was an *evil touch* on my left arm to impact my RELATIONSHIP with either the man who *I* believed to be my boyfriend, or the one that she believed or wanted to be *her* boyfriend. Obviously, they were the same person.

The human mind is amazing, especially a woman's mind. We can recall things that a man might not ever think was important. We can even put dates and *times* on the events in our recall. It's a gift; pretty much every woman has it.

I recall without asking, early into my relationship with Mr. Smell Good him telling me he left an office social event to go to the witch's home *for a drink*. As far as I know he's never called her a witch, and he might not know she's one. When one is bewitched one of the purposes is to blind the person to the fact that they are dealing with a witch.

Why you leave a place with *drinks* to go for a *drink* is somewhat obvious to another woman, plainly obvious to a man with a plan, and blatantly obvious to the *witch* who planned it.

This person lives with her mother, who is also a witch. I'm not being judgmental here; the child of a witch is **automatically** a witch. The spouse of a witch is considered a witch; you two are **one**. Careful…

In his visit to their home, he told me, without my asking, that they had a special chair for him to sit in and he sat there. They gave him a glass of red wine; he hates red wine. Then her mother brought him a piece of red velvet cake; he hates red velvet cake. Monochromatic witchcraft: who knew that was a thing? Those with even a little imagination can guess why everything was **RED**.

At the time of this "confession," I'd met this man once and was not too invested right then. Then he told me he fell asleep in the chair. Now, I only imagine the chair also being red, but what do I know? And what did any of that have to do with me? Okay, I'm thinking to myself, this guy is honest to the *extreme*? Maybe he's trustworthy? *Anyhoo*-- glad he told me, though, so I could put this all together later on.

Thank You, Holy Spirit for bringing this back to my memory and also for Wisdom to apply the knowledge that I already have so I know what to do with the information.

All those red moves at her house were witchcraft moves for those who don't know. We might talk about it later—not sure…

# *Love*, In the Time of COVID

What was I doing at the time of this *visitation*? COVID had just been defined, so I, like millions, was relegated to being at home at 2:30 in the afternoon sleeping on some random weekday, bored. Wondering why I was home. Well, the Governor of the state had said to stay home.

Anyway, I needed sleep because for the 18 months prior, I was up 2 or 3 hours longer than usual EVERY night on the phone with Mr. Smell Good, either on FaceTime or an audio call.

Like clockwork. He called me first thing every morning and every night. He was delightful; we talked all the way to work and back, we texted, called, talked and *meme'd* each other all day. Our conversation was continuous, it never stopped; we spent the entire day together, every day, even though we lived hours apart. He sent me love songs. He sent me long stemmed red roses, two dozen at a time. He wrote me a love letter or a beautiful hand-written card which I received also like clockwork in my real mailbox on Wednesdays because jokingly I had told him I only go to the mailbox on Wednesdays.

When I saw him, I touched neither my wallet, nor any doors, or any chair in any restaurant. Was he perfect for me? Pretty much. We were in a full-blown relationship that was fully blowing my mind. It was almost too much attention, like being love-bombed, but then I decided that I liked it.

But what was I *really* doing? **I was sinning**. I was in *sin-fun* with a person who was a barrel of laughs and rather put together. It was very exciting.

Oh, and he could pray some tight prayers. So, I thought he was a *mand* of God….and this was some new kind of balance of spirituality and *life* that I had never seen before. He was fun, attentive, good looking, smart, successful, and he smelled really good. Yeah, that's what I was doing. Take out all the adjectives that described *him* and you will know that I was *sinning*. Not proud of it.

You know we are under Grace right now. But we should not use Grace as an opportunity to sin. Me, included. Thankfully, God is Merciful.

Every day, tender mercies. In our seasons of *fun*, we wake up the next morning and nothing in the PHYSICAL has happened to us, so we either think what we did yesterday was OKAY, and/or nothing is going to happen to us. We may think that God is OK with sin.

**He's not.**

When we sin, the glory of God leaves us. So, as I describe the visiting witch as *Ichabod*, where had my own glory gone?

# Not In the Physical

Note, I said, nothing in the **physical** happened to us. I didn't say nothing in the *spiritual* happened.

Back then while in the State of Ignorance something in the *spiritual* DID happen, loud and in person and I looked at it and reported it and behaved as if it was a movie that I played a part in--, almost like it was happening to someone else and not me.

More ignorance.

Ask the Lord for more Grace, there's already too much ignorance going around.

It was **not** a movie; it was my REAL life. It was my real, *spiritual* life. And what happened, actually happened. Whether I believed *in* it or not; it happened. Whether I know what to call it or not: it happened. Whether I told anyone or not, it happened. Whether I understood it or not, it happened. Whether I did nothing or did something about it; it happened. It happened in the *spiritual*, **so it happened**.

Men ought to always pray. If God is so gracious to show you something in the spiritual, it's because He loves you. He gives you time to **command** that thing, to either pray it into existence as in a prophetic word, or to **stop it** by prayer, fasting, decree, and declaration from coming into existence if it is something negative, such as an **evil touch** with an *evil intent*.

An uninvited, evil visitation with evil intent is quite an afternoon—even in the boring days of COVID lockdown. What you do about an evil *visitation* and an *evil touch* depends on your Salvation, your spiritual maturity, understanding and knowledge. What you do about it depends on your willingness to pray. What you don't do about it depends on your level of **ignorance,** stubbornness, laziness, and your awareness to even *think* you need to do anything about it.

# It Takes Time

This thing that happened in the spiritual may take a little time or a lot of time to get to the physical. It may not happen immediately in the physical, but then again, it may.

If it takes *time* to get from the spiritual to the physical, that's when we know we're under some Amazing Grace. God gives us a Grace period between this and that, between cause and effect, between **sin** and death, really. He gives us time to repent. And, that's Love.

Just as in the natural, there's a grace period between a certain requirement--, like a payment and if that requirement or payment is not met on time, then something untoward may happen.

Grace is always a good thing, but we should not use it as an opportunity to sin. But humans do. I did; Lord, hear my cry of repentance and forgive me.

In my line of work, I have heard many people say they woke up sick. Did evil, spiritual things happen last night, or overnight to them? Or did something evil happen to them some time ago and then just *manifested* in the natural today? It depends.

I am saved, and by Jesus Christ I'm under Grace. The person who wakes up sick who was attacked spiritually in the night who has a physical manifestation the very next morning – perhaps they weren't saved, or they were saved but prayerless and careless, as in the driest of dry seasons and haven't prayed since forever. Perhaps they've been buffeted time and time again, in the dream, in the night. Fed *spirit* food over and over until a sickness manifested. One last *spirit* meal or snack and the precipice was reached last night, then this morning they are sick.

Perhaps they were a reprobate soul. Perhaps their sickness at daybreak was a witch-on-sinner crime so because of sin, a person may be wide open to occultic attack.

Please note that under God's Grace of which I speak, witchcraft which is most often *occultic*, that is *hidden* or unseen, a surprise attack, wasn't occultic to me. God, by His Holy Spirit clearly showed me what the small, lightless woman in black was up to.

# What Did You Dream?

Dreams to scatter good things from your life come as attacks even against *prayed up* Christians. They more easily come up against prayerless and carnal Christians, and **sinners**. We all have sinned and come short of the Glory of God; if we say we haven't, we are lying. Dreams that bring demotion to your life present in the night. There are dreams that limit destiny, dreams that bring stagnation, sickness, backwardness, and/or poverty. While men sleep, the enemy sows weeds (Matthew 13:25). The devil doesn't want you to have successes or anything good, including relationships, marriages, and Godly children.

Dreams intended to break up relationships happen to people. Dreams and *visitations* of **evil touch** happen to people, usually in the night or anytime in their sleep; even if it's 2:00 pm in the afternoon. I say happen to people because if you have a bad dream and *do nothing about it*, what you dreamed or what the dream meant will come to pass in your life. Dreams that steal, kill or destroy are sent from the Evil One from one, more or all of his three channels, Steal, Kill and Destroy.

God gives people dreams to alert, protect, and to prod you to action.

> Then, after doing all those things, I will pour out my Spirit upon all people. Your sons and daughters will prophesy. Your old men will dream dreams, and your young men will see visions. (Joel 2:28 NLT)

You MUST have proper Christian, Biblical dream interpretation of whatever you dream. The worldly online stuff spins dream interpretations into *happy*. If you have only favorable dream interpretations-- even if it was a tornado, earthquake, and a flood all rolled into one, you will be at ease and do nothing, when you should be doing a whole lot of ***something***. Doing nothing is what will make you a victim. For example, dreams where someone takes your car, your shoes; are intended to hinder or stop your ministry.

*Who knew?*

Eating food and or having sex in the dream defiles a person. A defiled person is the forerunner of a condemned person. A person who sins, even if it is *fun*-sin is **DEFILED**. A defiled person is easy to attack, spiritually. Being condemned is the last step before destruction.

Three channels: Steal, Kill & Destroy—remember that.

# The Touch of God

Healing, deliverance, wholeness, hope, anointing, joy, peace, and favor are some of the reasons why we want the *touch* of God. We flourish by touch. Babies who are not touched do not thrive. Touch can edify, touch can anoint, touch can build up. Divine touch can heal, it can uplift, it can protect. Divine touch can anoint, impart, it can bring life. Human touch is needed for life, but a Divine touch from God is **everything**. So, we seek not only the *face* of God, we want His countenance upon us, but we aspire to divine touch.

Conversely, we may have deduced through just living that people will do all kinds of things. The evil hands that employ **evil touch**, also do other kinds of evil with those wicked hands.

# Evil Handwriting

The hand is supposed to be a life shaping tool to pave your way to fulfilling Godly destiny. With your hands, you knock so divine doors will be opened unto you. You hold your life, loves, family and destiny in your hands. Your hands touch the Mercy of God through repentance. And, God says we can come boldly to the Throne of Grace to obtain Mercy.

The Hand of God blesses us, it blesses the land, and it blesses the works of our own hands. The hands of the angels bless and keep us. *On their hands they will bear you up, so that you will not strike your foot against a stone*, (Psalm 91, Luke 4:11).

We lift up Holy hands before the Lord, indicating that we have no weapons. It indicates surrender to the Most High God. Holy Hands are Righteous hands, they are hands that praise and

Worship God. They are hands that God blesses. God extends Hands of Mercy toward us when we seek Him with a contrite spirit and a penitent heart.

Conversely, the hand of Satan employs ***evil touch***. The dark hearts who use the dark arts misuse everything, but the hands are especially wicked.

Wicked people are behind evil handwriting, which is s form of curse-making. Evil hands write evil things against people in the realm of the spirit. But we have protection by the Blood of Jesus; we just have to seek it, and open our mouth and pray.

> Blotting out the handwriting of ordinances that was against us, which was contrary to us, and took it out of the way, nailing it to his cross;
> (Colossians 2:14)

There are evil, lying documents in the spirit. *Spirit spouse* has an evil, lying marriage certificate stating that some unsuspecting human married *it* most likely in the dream, while *it* was *dressed* as a human in a masquerade. Unless the memory of the *spirit* marriage is completely wiped from the human's mind.

There are evil divorce decrees which the enemy is trying to make, prophetically to break up real Earth marriages. The devil accuses man 24/7 before God and will make and record evil judgements against mankind. None of this could be true, but if the devil or any of his evil, human agents can get a person to believe and repeat any of his lies, that man is then on the path to fulfilling the evil prophecy. If he is spiritually ignorant and has a big, uncontrolled mouth, he can do a lot of damage to his own life.

**Immediate Prayer Points:**

Blood of Jesus, wash away, blot out all evil handwriting against my life, in the Name of Jesus.

Evil verdicts, be expunged from every evil record against me, all marine verdicts, witchcraft verdicts, all *familiar* and *monitoring spirit* verdicts, be blotted out in Jesus' Name. Lord, perfect the matters of my life and overturn all evil handwriting and verdicts against me, in Jesus' Name.

**Do Not Sign Anything in Your Dream.**

Any handwriting of mine, any signature of mine on any evil document in the spirit or in the natural, be blotted out by the Blood of Jesus, in Jesus' Name.

Handwriting of God. Rewrite my story; restore my glory. Divine pen of God, write, cancel or rewrite my destiny and success, in the Name of Jesus.

**Prayer for Hands**

Father, thank You for filling my hands with life, good success and miracles.

Hands of the wicked, forcing goods out of my hands, wither and perish.

Father, deliver me from the hands of the night. Deliver me from the hands of the wicked. Deliver me from captivity and from my captors. Deliver me from the hands of sin. Deliver me from the hands of ignorance, stupidity and rebellion, in the Name of Jesus.

Lord, deliver me from the hands of JEALOUSY.

Hell, hath no fury like a scorned, rejected, jealous woman. It's sad to be soul tied to someone who doesn't even want you. The Lord has better for us all. The Ichabod-*ish* woman who visited me *may be* **that man's physical, spirit spouse**. I may have thought it was his "wife" because she may have married him, in the spirit. *Goes into equals* married, people. Witches become a satanic altar which he may or may not know that *he* did or still worships at. She believes he is hers. Oddly, she has a covenant with *him*, and no covenant with me. Why she thought she should punish *me* for **him** breaking their soul-tie or weird covenant is a question for the ages; most scorned women think this way.

- Every curse operating against my life, die.
- Every evil covenant against my life, break! I cancel the iniquity and the effect of these curses and covenants, with the Blood of Jesus, in the Name of Jesus.

# Evil Hands

Thieves roam about this Earth; they have since time immemorial. They do damage in the natural. Since leaving the **State of Ignorance**, I've learned that evil hands roam about in the spirit with the intent to steal, kill, and destroy. Hidden and left unchecked, they can do a lot of damage for a lot of years, while the victim doesn't even know he's under attack. Living a life of frustration and defeat, one may blame their miserable life on "the man," "the system", racism, sexism, ageism. Blaming one of those *-isms*, a person is choosing something that is SO BIG that he thinks there is nothing he/she can do about it, so they do nothing about it. They just suffer and live a *less-than* kind of life.

If they only knew that their lives were being systematically dismantled by the power and ill-intent of the hands of one solitary, dull-looking person, individually, or a coven, collectively working against them. *Ichabods* have lost the glory of God because they employ the power of Satan. If we only knew, realized and remembered that we have authority over all that, and we can shut it down. We can shut them down by the Power of Christ Jesus and live the abundant life that Jesus came and died for us to have.

Evil hands come to steal, kill, destroy, snatch, and scatter good things from your life. And they come to transfer disaster into your body, relationships, marriage, business, education, profession. Arrows shot are arrows of affliction or death, to divert destiny or do any and all of the above.

The **evil touch** of evil hands tries to press down your head when you are sleeping, to steal from you in the dream. I had a dream where a strongman cashier took my wallet. I snatched it back from him. How dare he! Plus, it was my purple wallet; that's **MINE**!

Your spirit man has to really be built up to defend your life in real time within the dream. When evil hands try to snatch your money, valuables, wallet, spouse, children, wedding ring, shoes, garments-- **NO, they can't have any of**

**that**. Yes, because it's yours, but also because of what each item *represents* in the spiritual and in the natural.

Evil hands have shot people with guns in their dreams. They've stabbed and injected folks--, none of this is good. Do something about it! The *evil touch* of evil hands intends to bring you shame, reproach, rejection, even death. They want to contaminate and pollute your reputation and life. **Pregnant couples, your warfare is intense.** KEEP EVIL HANDS OFF YOUR BELLY, WOMB, AND BABY. Yes, in the spirit, *and* in the natural.

Some other *evil touch*/evil hand dream attacks are rotten fruit, pouring ink to stain white things such as paper or garments. The powers behind *evil touch* are witchcraft, wicked powers, terminating powers, evil priests, and sorcerers.

**Immediate Prayer Point:**

Every evil priest ministering against me at any evil altar, be burnt to ashes along with your altar, in the Name of Jesus.

# You Are *Not* in Good Hands

Satanic evil human agents lay hands on the innocent and unsuspecting. People of God, the question, *"Can I have a hug?"* is echoing in my mind, so I must tell you, huggers beware. I'm not saying you shouldn't be warm and friendly, but not to everyone. Use, *"There's COVID, or I'm not a hugger,"* excuse. Say whatever you need to, but don't let folks put their hands on you, unless you have release from the Holy Spirit—**especially** if you're pregnant.

Destiny killer *spirits* come in people that you would never suspect. Yes, **evil touch** can be done in the dream, but **evil touch** is also a real thing in the natural:

- Satanic barbers and hair stylists.
- Demonic pastors and priests
- False prophets
- Fake church folks--, evil pew mates

- Wicked parents
- Evil bosses
- Evil co-workers
- Evil co-eds/schoolmates

These types could be glory exchangers or stealers. They could be spiritual thieves working with *graveyard spirits*, the *spirit of death and hell*, or others. They may not be working with any *spirit*; they could just be evil. If you experience a dark shadow in your dream that touches you, better get to praying.

**Immediate Prayer Point**:

Every dark shadow, every power pursuing me with the *spirit of death or spirit of the graveyard*, you die! Die! Die. I will not die, but I will live and declare the goodness of the Lord, in the Land of the Living. What you intended for me--, you have it. Die, in the Name of Jesus.

Evil marine kingdom powers send agents after you, especially in the dream—such as strongmen, enchanters, diviners, *familiar spirits, a*ncestral powers, star gazers, and dream attackers. The *spirit of Balaam* comes to curse people.

*(Min. Joshua Orekhie is one of the finest Biblical dream interpreters, ever. He has topical videos on YouTube.* https://evangelistjoshua.com/breaking-stronghold-evil-hands)

## Prayer Point:

Every evil hand that I am unaware of that I receive needed or desired services from, be cut off from your evil power source, wither and die and have no future effect on me, in the Name of Jesus. Every evil handed doctor, dentist, nurse, barber, hair stylist, masseuse, coach, physical therapist-- anyone, your evil touches against me are nullified today and forever by the Power of Christ. In the Name of Jesus Christ, we pray. Amen.

# Can We Pray Yet?

To know how to pray against this, we need to learn a bit more. The Addams Family, **Thing** was a disembodied hand. Movies and TV shows can be very telling if we pay close, spiritual attention. The Addams family is an example of spooky evil, so a touch from that *Thing* would never be desirable. Neither is demonic ***evil touch*** desirable in any of our lives in the dream or in the natural.

**In your dreams** if you have experienced any of the following, the evil hands demons are at work against you.

- Being arrested and handcuffed.
- Shackles on your feet.
- Having your diplomas and certificates stolen or destroyed.

- Have you seen your name on an evil list?
- Have you ever been slimed or had trash or garbage dumped on you in the dream?
- Defiled by urine, feces or the blood of animals?
- Dragged in mud?

All of this is *defilement*.

Has your hair ever been cut off in the dream? That happened to me in a dream once. It was only a little trim, but I demanded that they PUT MY HAIR BACK AND I INSISTED UNTIL MY HAIR WAS PUT BACK, REATTACHED. Hey, it's a dream and it's *my* dream. My spirit man is running this.

If your soul was running your dream life, and you got an evil haircut, you may have become sad and cried. If your flesh was running the dream, your response to the haircut may have been that you cussed somebody out. Yeah, let the spirit man run things. Be sure you are prayed up and you feed your spirit man daily, and you are well connected to the Holy Spirit of God.

Evil hands can use brooms to scatter or sweep away your destiny, glory, career, marriage, children, happiness, and et cetera. You've got real praying to do, people of God!

**Prayer Points**:

Every witchcraft broom assigned against me to scatter my life, die – you and your sweeper: I bind you and I paralyze you from ever sweeping against me or my life again, in the Name of Jesus. If the sweeper is innocent and unknowingly put on task by a real witch, Lord, have Mercy on the innocent and draw them to salvation. I cancel every incantation of the real witch, and evil spell and demons associated with it, BACK TO SENDER!!!

No reason to be afraid of your doctor, dentist or phlebotomist, it's the dream injectors that you need to be concerned about. Evil hands give evil injections and sometimes they draw blood from you in the dream! The purpose of this is to pollute your blood and put sickness, illnesses and incurable diseases in you.

This is not a movie, *peeps*. Watch for dream "people" with weapons such as knives, or broken glass.

Evil hands may try to put evil marks on a victim. These marks are to single a person out for destruction, death, reproach, rejection, hatred, and/or affliction.

Worse, evil hands sometimes want to bring something horrible to the Earth and into your life. Those evil plans must be aborted.

- Evil hands behind evil pregnancies in my life, wither now, you shall not come to term, in the Name of Jesus.

I was receiving deliverance one day and had such a violent reaction when the Apostle called out padlocks that it was unreal. Evil hands are behind padlocks against a person's life. Padlocks are to block the flow of money, finances, career, business, marriage, and the reproductive organs. Saints of God we MUST have proper dream interpretation because a week or so after that deliverance I had another padlock dream, but it WAS NOT a bad dream, it was amazing, actually. So, we must either properly interpret dreams or know someone who can.

The Holy Spirit can always tell you exactly what your dream means in. Write your dreams down and pray them back to the Holy Spirit line by line and let Him tell you what the dream means, how to pray and what to do about it.

**Immediate Prayer Points**:

Every satanic programmer, programming evil into my life, catch fire, and crash, in the Name of Jesus.

I sign nothing in the dream, no evil contracts, covenants, certificates, invoices, receipts of any kind, in the Name of Jesus.

Anything I have signed in the past, Blood of Jesus blot my name and signature off any and every evil document whether I signed it knowingly, or whether I was tricked into signing anything, in the Name of Jesus.

Lord, render the signatures of my ancestors on any evil document NULL & VOID. I repent for them, and I receive the blessings of my bloodline, but I do not receive the iniquity of their sins, in Jesus' Name.

I reject every dream receipt, contract or paper handed to me in the dream, in the Name of Jesus.

What's on a receipt or a contract handed to you in a dream? You may not know. **DO NOT ACCEPT anything FROM AN EVIL OR UNKOWN ENTITY in the dream, unless you KNOW you are snatching back something**

**they've stolen from you**. A dream document could be a bill for something your ancestors received eons ago. It could be a headstone receipt for your own burial. You need to go to sleep prayed up because in devil world, everything is a trap.

Evil hands come to do evil exchange of things such as your stars, glory, destiny, future, marriage, children, wealth--, you name it.

# It Don't Feel *Too Good*

Evil hands on your spiritual life may feel something like this to your natural life:

- Sorrow
- Bad luck
- Demotion
- Death
- Divorce
- Barrenness
- Impotence
- Confusion
- Wastefulness
- Sickness/Disease
- Torment
- Working hard, getting nowhere.

# Redemption & Reversal

Are you saved? Yes. Good. Holy Spirit filled? Yes. Even better. Repent to God. Renounce all sins. Break all sin covenants by the Blood of Jesus. Can you fast? Then do it and be prayerful as you fast.

**Pray:**

Lord, cover me in the Blood of Jesus.

Lord, I come to Your Throne of Grace to find help in this time of trouble. I pray for Mercy for myself, in the Name of Jesus. Lord, I ask judgment to be passed on my enemies, my unrepentant, perpetual enemies.

My life, receive Fire; become Fire, in the Name of Jesus.

Evil hands coming against me, and my life be cut off now, in the Name of Jesus.

All evil hands tampering with God's calendar for my life and/or my destiny clock, receive Holy Ghost Fire now, in the Name of Jesus.

Every evil hand of household wickedness upon my life, catch Fire now, in the Name of Jesus.

Every evil JEALOUS hand against my life, catch Fire now, in the Name of Jesus.

Every strongman in place to hinder my progress, be paralyzed and die, in the Name of Jesus.

Every devil assigned to enforce any curse against me or my bloodline, you are fired, go to the Abyss now, from where there is no return, in the Name of Jesus.

Every evil inheritance of my life, I reject you now, in the Name of Jesus.

Every evil inheritance of my life, die by the power in the Blood of Jesus.

Fire of God, fire every evil hand tying me down to one spot, in the Name of Jesus.

Every evil assignment of the enemy for my life, be terminated by Fire, in the Name of Jesus.

Every completed work of the enemy in my life be <u>undone</u> and destroyed and let all the evil effects be removed from my life and backfire on the sender(s), in the Name of Jesus.

Lord, stop the sun, stop the moon as You did for Joshua, Lord, redeem the time, restore the years. Clock of dreams, Clock of visitation REWIND and take me back to that time, timeline, moment, dimension and realm of that *evil touch* by the Ichabod witch who touched my elbow.

I undo it, I turn it around. I deprogram the curse and spell. I dismantle that *evil touch* and any and all spells the Ichabod witch, or any other witch, warlock, priest or priestess sent my way from my birth until right now, in the Name of Jesus. Take it back to them all, on the Whirlwind of God, in Jesus' Name.

I break and revoke every covenant in my life that opened any door that allowed her or any witch to come to me, in the Name of Jesus. I revoke every spell, chant, affirmation, incantation, hex, vex, or jinx behind any and all evil magic directed at me, in the Name of Jesus.

I break every bondage that allowed her to come to me, by the King of Glory. I nullify the evil energy behind the spell. I break the covenant keeping the spell in place. Blood of Jesus, speak for me, speak for me against the demon(s) behind every wretched spell cast against my life.

I revoke the spell; I revoke every curse and spell. I bind every demon used to enforce her or any evil intent upon my elbow, my body, my life, my health, my purpose, my destiny, my relationship(s), my ministry, and finances, by the Blood of Jesus.

Every demon, devil and curse involved in this and any spell: back to Sender, in the Name of Jesus.

I REVOKE every evil covenant, in the Name of Jesus.

Jehovah Sabaoth rebuke that power, that devil, that demon, those demons, every power of that witch in the Name of Jesus and prevent any part of her body, soul, or spirit, any of her witchcraft, curses, warfare, corruption, and evil from transferring to me and return it all fully upon her head, forever in every timeline, era, age, dimension and realm, in the Name of Jesus.

I separate her evil from its power source/sources, from its network and ask Lord for a power failure against her and every dark arts worker against me.

Lord, EXPOSE it, expose the evil human agent(s) operating against me both then, and also today, and everything in between, in the Name of Jesus.

Restore me, Lord to where I was *before* the visitation, or even better, by the Power of God and the Power of His Christ, in the Name of Jesus.

Powers siphoning my blessings, you have been found out. Warrior Angels of God, spoil their strongman/strongmen, and every evil entity, after you repay me SEVEN-FOLD, catch Fire, fall down and die, in the Name of Jesus.

I bind the *spirit of retaliation*. Every power-seeking counterattack as a result of these prayers, hear a terrifying noise from Heaven, and scatter unto desolation, by the God of Elijah.

Evil hand(s) assigned against me, every evil intent against me, I bind you, and I break your connection with all your demonically organized networks in the spiritual and in the physical world. Be wasted and put to shame, in Jesus' Name.

Every wicked agenda of death and hell against my life, the Lord Jesus Christ has defeated you; you have no authority to do any of that to me. Retreat and fall down and die, in the Name of Jesus.

Every monitoring ear, eye or device, go monitor yourself and leave my presence forever, lose my coordinates and forget my location forever, in the Name of Jesus. Thank You Lord, it is done!

# Let's Pray

The ***evil touch*** of the enemy comes to steal, kill, and destroy. The left side, the right side--, what was touched and also where you were touched has implications. If your hands have been touched/cursed, if a spell or curse has been issued against your hands, you need to pray very well against that.

**Pray These Prayers**:

Blood of Jesus, terminate every satanic curse on my hands, in the Name of Jesus.

Every evil generational covenant that affects my hands, break today, by the power in the Blood of Jesus.

Every verdict, sentence, or curse on my hands in the Spirit realm be reversed by the power, in the Blood of Jesus.

Every Satanic glove or covering preventing my hands from prosperity, catch Fire, burn to ashes and disintegrate, in Jesus' Name.

Every mark of negativity on my hand be expunged now, by the Blood of Jesus.

Every satanic hole in my hands or pockets siphoning off or causing me to waste or lose money, be sealed by the power in Jesus' Blood.

Every *spirit of death* residing in my hands making me unsuccessful in life, be consumed by Holy Ghost Fire, in Jesus' Name.

Every satanic impartation that has rendered my hand dead, I cancel you now, by the power in the Blood of Jesus.

Every Covenant of dead hands and dead Destiny break off my hands, in the Name of Jesus.

Every foundational power consigned to stop my work and stagnate destiny, fail now, in Jesus' Name.

Every strong man of my father's or mother's house, assigned to stop the work of my hands, be paralyzed by Fire, in the Name of Jesus.

Every strong man over any ex's house, or any relative's, friend's, enemy's, fake friend's, co-worker's or co-ed's house, on assignment to stop my progress, be paralyzed by Holy Ghost Fire now, in the Name of Jesus.

Every power of *evil touch* attacking the work of my hand be canceled post haste, in Jesus' Name.

Every demonic attacker sent to paralyze the work of my hands, by Fire by Force, I will not be stopped; you freeze, in the Name of Jesus.

Every demonic poison in my hand responsible for misfortunes in my life, be neutralized by the Blood of Jesus.

Every spiritual draining pipe connected to my hands be disconnected and shattered by the Thunder Hammer of God. Lord, heal every defect in my hand spiritually, and in the natural, in the Name of Jesus.

Every evil arrow hat has struck my hand, wasting my efforts, come out today and catch Fire, in Jesus' Name.

Divine Saws of God, cut asunder every padlock locking away my blessings, destiny, destiny helpers, and relationships. Spoil every strongman. Angels of God, retrieve my blessings for me, in Jesus' Name.

Every stubborn enemy delegated to render me jobless. I judge you today by the Word of God. Die, in the Name of Jesus.

Every mark of redundancy upon my palm, disappear today, by Fire, in the Name of Jesus.

Every promise and prospect falling through my hands stop now and be restored back to me, in Jesus' Name.

Every project in my hands that has stopped as a result of dead hands, my hands and the project-- be resurrected now, by the Resurrection Power of Christ.

Every prosperous relationship that has been terminated because of cursed hands be revived again, renewed, resurrected, in Jesus' Name.

Every satanic hole in my hands, leaking wealth, riches and prosperity, be healed and sealed by the Blood of Jesus.

Anointing of God to rest upon my hand now and propel my life forward, in Jesus' Name. Anointing, fall on me.

You, my hands. I command you to prosper in all areas of my life, in Jesus' Name.

My hands, receive the strength of God and prosper, in the Name of Jesus. Angel of the Living God, revive my hands today, in the Name of Jesus.

Holy Ghost Fire strengthen my hands today for job, career, and prosperity, in the Name of Jesus.

By the wind of Heaven, I command my dead hands to resurrect, in the Name of Jesus. From today I receive new hands for a profitable job, profitable career, profitability and prosperity, abundance, and no lack, in the Name of Jesus.

I declare and decree that the works of my hands prosper by Divine mandate, in Jesus's Name.

My hands, be delivered today from the curse of fruitlessness, barrenness, and non-productivity, in Jesus' Name.

My hands, prosper, be fruitful, be productive, and multiply by the Word of God, in the Name of Jesus.

Lord God, let your prophecy for my successful hands come into manifestation, in Jesus' Name.

Lord God, let the work of the Kingdom prosper in my hands, in the Name of Jesus.

Thank You, Lord God, for answering my prayers, in the Name of Jesus. Amen.

# You're Pulling My Leg

A touch on the left elbow or arm is to interfere in relationships--, marriage. A touch on the right elbow/arm would be to affect finances. People have experienced touches in their sleep and in the dream, that feel like a **real touch** on any of the places that I've mentioned or anywhere else on the body.

You didn't imagine this.

An **evil touch** or a pull on the leg is to affect where a person walks, and it affects their destiny, wealth, and successes. Saved man or woman of God, **you** have the knowledge and the weapons to fight when the enemy attacks. This is not the time to ask someone to pray for you; it's past time you pray for yourself. You can't ask someone to take a shower *for* you. In the same way, you've got to pray against, and put to rest, the defilement, the evil, the reproach, the spell, curse, and the spiritual funk off of you, yourself.

Man, who has a tendency to forget, may not connect cause and effect if there is a time delay between an *evil touch* and an unfortunate outcome in his life. Even though it is God's Grace that allows *time* between an *evil touch* and some physical disaster in his life. So, he may not be able to put together the cause and effect of things. It's better to have the grace period than not; thank You, Lord. But if man doesn't put it together, he may not believe that something spiritual really caused something natural. But it happens that way every day.

Witches can program curses against your feet. Witches deploy *foot track magic*, using the soil you stepped on, the shoe or footprint you left in the dirt, even tire tracks, like they are CSI agents. They will even take the dirt from the bottom of your shoe. The 1970's song, **The Cleanup Woman's** lyrics may allow us to now understand *how she was able to take everyone's man*. She had their *dirt* and their DNA.

The evil purpose of pulling the leg is to cause poverty to come into a person's life. It can affect where you go in life; it can keep you from divine connections and divine destinations. You may not ever meet your destiny helpers or be in the right place at the right times, impacting relationships, marriages, career, or whether you have the children you are **supposed to have**.

In the dream, or in the night, if you feel a pressure or weight on your feet, that is sent to bring stagnation to your life. Fight it. Don't be like a stubborn mule standing still but you don't even know why. **Force** yourself into action or back into action. Ramp up your prayers. *(Leg prayers after this section.)*

Leg curses have caused people to walk away from their family and they don't know why. Their picture is on a milk carton because their family can't find them. The curse programmed them to walk away from their spouse and/or family, or to walk *toward* someone else. Listen: With little to no God onboard, the victim simply obeyed the voice of evil. When a person is not saved, they have a contract, a covenant, and agreement with the devil, and they do what the devil tells them to do. Although they may swear that they don't. They do.

You, yourself have had annoying suggestions or instructions from the devil, but you were strong enough to resist. The unsaved, the carnal Christian, the fake-saved, will not have the strength to resist.

**There is deep spiritual stuff happening in the world 24/7. If you have no spiritual covering, no spiritual protection, why do you even bother to lock the door of your house at night?**

You can suspect an attack on your legs or feet if you have heavy legs, aching legs, aching feet, suddenly or for no real reason. PRAY against witchcraft. Heel pain, plantar fasciitis, bunions and bone spurs are common foot disorders--, PRAY. The heart of man is deceitfully wicked, the person(s) sending the curse could be a sibling, fake friend, and smiling in your face every day. There are so many ways for a person to render a curse whether they be a wizard, warlock, witch or a blind witch.

I know more than one person who can't sit still, they can't stay home; that is also a curse against feet. Pray against a *vagabond spirit*, a *nomadic spirit*. God desires stability in His people; He strengthens and establishes us. He may send us out for missions and for other reasons, but stability is important to God. People who are unstable in all their ways cannot be blessed of God.

**Break the Curse**

When witches are against you or hired against you, sometimes they target the legs. Are you habitually late everywhere you go? Suspect that your legs may have been spiritually tampered with by evil human agents. You cannot use that as an excuse at work, but it will give insight into how to pray about your life.

If there is a curse on your legs, when it is broken, your life will get so much better. Your legs/feet could have been touched, tagged, tied, roped or padlocked. Exactly what an enchanter said can be known by the Spirit, but if it is not known, then pray as the Spirit leads you, shows you, or gives you utterance.

If in a dream you are captured or defeated, pray for deliverance of your leg(s). If you are flying in your dream, pray for deliverance of the leg, immediately. If you have constant battles for your marriage, job, ministry, children, you need deliverance of the leg.

Capturing the leg is how the victim ends up on remote control. If you can't tell yourself or your spouse why you went to a certain place and you keep going there, you could be on remote control by the enemy.

**Fire Prayers for the Leg**

Holy Ghost Fire, fall. My life, receive Fire, become Fire. Lord, make me too hot for my enemies, in Jesus' Name.

Trap of backwardness that has captured my leg, break by Fire, in the Name of Jesus.

Arrow of not being in the right place at the right time, or on time, fired into my leg, come out by Fire, in Jesus' Name.

Witchcraft enchantment attachment to my legs, break by Fire, in the Name of Jesus.

Whosoever is hunting for my leg, die in shame, in the Name of Jesus.

By Fire, by Thunder, every curse, break, break, break!

Stagnancy and delay affecting my life, break now, in the Name of Jesus.

Demons of paralysis and stroke, my leg is not for you. Release my leg now, in Jesus' Name. (X3)

Diseases and stubborn infirmity, release my leg, and die, in Jesus' Name.

Demonic chains keeping me from good success, I command you to break by Thunder, in Jesus' Name.

Arrows of laziness and lateness in my leg come out now by Fire, in Jesus' mighty Name.

My legs, I command you to reach out to the people and take me to places of Godly success in my life, in Jesus's Name.

Any power or force trying to drive me into a storm, be discomfited by the Lightning of God, then die by Fire, in the Name of Jesus.

Thunder of God, ROLL! Break every bewitchment over my life, in the Name of Jesus.

Problems that entered my life, through **evil touch**—of my foot, my leg, or through foot track magic. I cancel you now, in the Name of Jesus. I command you to leave, and never come back, in the Name of Jesus. Return to sender.

Wings of destruction given to me so that I would fly in my dream, Fire of God burn those wings; burn them to total destruction, melt them like the wax of Icarus. Angels of Protection, bear me up so I do not fall or receive any harm, in Jesus' Name.

Warrior Angels with your powerful wings knock every evil power out of my life forever, in the Name of Jesus.

Python pollution, cursing, itching in my palm, I bury you in the Blood of Jesus. Curse and spell of poverty on my hand, elbow, arm, leg, foot, be broken now, in the Name of Jesus.

Poverty or any spell to destroy good things in my life or business, release me and be destroyed in Jesus' Name.

Every invisible giant holding my leg, foot, any body part, and lording over my life, I command you to fail against this servant of the Most High God. Fall down and die, in the Name of Jesus.

My feet, my legs, you are anointed for glory to God, for destiny and purpose and success, in Jesus' Name.

Shackles, chains, ropes, zip ties, or padlocks on my feet--, I crush every fetter, chain, iron, padlock--, any device to spiritually bind my legs or feet by the Thunder Hammer of God. Feet, legs, regain your freedom now, in Jesus' Name. Whom the Son sets free, is free, indeed.

Anointing of failure from hell, trying to flow on my legs or feet, I abruptly stop your flow; your time is expired, right now, in the Name of Jesus.

Charm in any *Evil Touch* that grabbed my legs, feet, or any part of my body, come out and die, in the Name of Jesus.

I soak my feet in the Blood of Jesus. I soak my feet in the anointing of God. I soak my feet in the purposes of the Lord. My feet are shod with the the Gospel of Peace. I offer peace and if it is not received, I shake the dust. I take back my Peace and I declare Peace and prosperity to *my* feet, my legs and my life, to the Glory of God. Amen.

I bury my hands in the Blood of Jesus.

Strange hand snatching good things from me – STOP! I can, I do, and I will have nice things. You have no authority over what My Father does for me or gives me. I snatch back everything that belongs to me, (7 times).

Strange and evil hand, dry up and wither, in the Name of Jesus.

Destiny helpers, my hands are anointed to receive from you; locate me now, in Jesus' Name.

Any power forcing good things out of my hands, you are terminated now, in the Name of Jesus.

# Sleep Paralysis

In my 20's, years before this *visitation,* long before I ever met the man that smelled really good and who was very attentive to me, I would blissfully go to bed but sometime in the night I would feel the bed go down, and it would wake me up, but there was no one there. Back then, I'd have what seemed like a thousand dreams. I could tell you five or six vivid dreams in the morning. But I didn't record them because I remembered them all. Neither did I get Christian, Biblical interpretation. It was more on the worldly side of dream interpretation, then. All the interpretations were happy, lucky, and fortunate so there was no *need* to pray a whole lot. But that was ALL A LIE. I was still in the **State of Ignorance** in my 20's-- book smart, but spiritually ignorant.

Being ignorant, I didn't know what the bed going down or feeling the sensation of the bed going down meant. When this happens, the bed is moving, but you're not. You can't. You want to call on Jesus, but your mouth won't move. You imagine your mouth is moving, but it's not, and no sound is coming out of you. Was it something to be concerned about? And not knowing if I was in a dream or if I was partially awake or all the way awake when this was happening was concerning. I just didn't know.

The department store incident obviously wasn't my first spiritual *visitation*. Lord, GOD, help me!

Ignorance is no excuse, however. God does not want us ignorant, so we can deduce that the devil *does* want us ignorant. The ignorant, the rebellious, and the sinful are the devil's favorite victims. When you look back on what you didn't know, thought you knew, or got completely wrong in your youth, you should praise God for all the things He has protected you from, kept you from and kept from you in all your youthful lust, ignorance, arrogance, and stupidity.

> My people are destroyed for a lack of knowledge. (Hosea 4:6)

So, the devil has three modes; Steal, Kill, and Destroy, with destroy being his ideal choice and outcome. Lacking knowledge will lead to destruction. Lacking knowledge is dangerous for humans so this book is to help you not be ignorant like I was. It's to keep you from doing *nothing* when you should be doing **something**. And it's so you won't do the wrong thing when you should do the right thing.

It's for when you have a spiritual dilemma, you don't tell just anyone, because the most spiritual person you know may not be spiritual *enough*, or spiritual at all. Or you tell the wrong someone and they tell you everything is fine, or everything is great, like when you make a customer service call to ANY company, and the agent on the other end tells you, *No problem* throughout the whole call, but never really helps you.

Sleep paralysis is a serious spiritual phenomenon that is explained away by medical science, saying that during REM sleep a person is *atonic,* believing they are awake, but they cannot move or speak.

During this time people report seeing figures of monsters, which science calls hallucinations. A spiritual person would call those demons or *spirits*. So, people believe there are no monsters, or spiritual wickedness or anything like that because God made an entire universe and populated *one* planet.

*Yeah, right.*

Science says that sometimes your brain inadvertently wakes up while your body is still under the "spell" of REM paralysis, leaving you stuck in a state between parallel realities. **So why is the bed going down? Why do you feel touch or pressure sensations against your physical body.** *Hello*? About that, I'd say the person wakes up in the flesh realm, but their spirit is still in the spirit realm experiencing *spiritual* things.

Egyptians (North Africa) say sleep paralysis is caused by *jinns* (genies) who are able to torment and kill their victims. Italians think it's caused by a mean witch called a *Pandafeche*, or a terrifying giant cat. In spiritual matters a cat represents witchcraft. In South Africa they believe it's caused by the black magic dwarf, *tokoloshe*. Turks believe is caused by *karabasan spirits* and Danes think it's just stress. From continent to continent and country to country, why do all those who experience sleep paralysis *see* or perceive similar stuff?

**Sleep paralysis is spiritual**. Medical science can only explain it away because many medical doctors and scientists, unfortunately, are not saved and not *spiritual*. Come at me if you want to--, most of the medical doctors I know are not saved. Most are also left brained and trained to think a certain way. They go to school for years to learn certain things and to think that certain way. If it can't fit in their head, it can't fit in their brain, it just won't. The things of God are spiritually discerned and understood.

The unspiritual don't build their spirit up to take charge of what presents in the dream, for example. So, they figure everything out in their great big brain that God gave them. In my 20's, I too, was book smart with little to no spiritual knowledge. The doctors I know are no longer in their 20's; we have all got to get spiritually wiser.

If you think that magic is cool, it's not; it is accomplished by demons. That's like sleep paralysis; magic acts work while you are suspended by some demonic charge; a demonic power has come over you. In a magic show, you think that's great. In sleep paralysis, you don't; you most often want to call for help. You want to call on the name of Jesus, but your mouth won't move, your vocal cords aren't making the sound you want. You feel as though your body won't move.

In my opinion, and this is strictly my opinion, **sleep apnea** maybe your body reacting to something that's happening to you in the *spirit* at night when your body is resting, and your soul is retrograde while your spirit man should be running things for the night. Everything that's happening to you at night is in the spirit, and your spirit man should be built up to handle the night shift.

If you're not saved, your spirit man is not built up. If you're low-key saved, doing just enough to fit in or not to stick out in a church crowd, your spirit man is not built up. If you're a lukewarm Christian, your spirit man is not built up. If you don't believe in things such as what I'm talking about, and things that really happen and you've not studied to show yourself approved, then your spirit man is not built up.

For all you know, sleep apnea could be you in captivity, being choked out. And sleep paralysis, much the same. Captivity, where they can do anything they want to you.

Ask God.

# The Womb

The womb is one of the most sacred places in the universe and it's in a human body. *Whew!* Witchcraft often tries to touch it, use it, exchange it; sometimes dark evil is successful. The devil does not want righteous seed coming forth. GOD does and God will have His way. God will bless the womb and the fruit of the body. God will make the womb fruitful as He told us to be fruitful and multiply.

*Evil touch* desires to abort good things in the womb, whether it be a woman's womb or the womb of the month, the year, of the entire Earth. Witchcraft wants to curse the womb, make it unfruitful and barren, or have it bring forth the most vile things. In the natural or in the dream an *evil touch* may be sent to do this. Whether you are pregnant or not, do not let random people touch you, your stomach, your womb (area) especially.

No matter why they say they want to touch it, don't let them. They don't need to feel your baby kick; is your baby a toy? There are all kinds of evil in the world.

There are all kinds of evil in the night, in your sleep, and in the dream. To dream of a touch on your stomach means that the enemy wants to contaminate, destroy or exchange your pregnancy. Getting pregnant, being pregnant, and bringing forth a healthy delivery is all warfare. *Evil touch* on your stomach area is the enemy trying to sow poverty or sorrow into your life. It means the devil is secretly stealing blessings from you and trying to destroy you with evil charms and enchantments.

**Prayer Points**

Demons of a barren womb, demons of miscarriage, any sterility, come out and die, in the Name of Jesus.

I plead the Blood of Jesus over my life and over my womb. My womb, open up and receive your miracle, in the Name of Jesus.

Illegal occupants in my womb, including witchcraft animals, or synthetic children, your time is up. Come out by Fire, in the Name of Jesus.

Finger of witches blocking my womb, wither by Fire, in the Name of Jesus.

My stolen or exchanged womb, come back to me. Come back home, in the Name of Jesus.

I drink the Blood of Jesus to heal my heart, my womb, and my life, in the Name of Jesus.

Witch's stone blocking my fallopian tubes, come out by Fire, in the Name of Jesus.

Strange fire burning in my womb, die, in the Name of Jesus.

Womb of good business ideas and vision to be successful in life, gestate for me now, in the Name of Jesus.

Hands of the Almighty God, rest upon my womb and start a new thing in me, in the Name of Jesus. Power of Jesus, fall upon my life and heal my womb. My womb, you are blessed, in the Name of Jesus.

Inflammation of the womb, be healed now, in the Name of Jesus, by the touch of God, by the Blood of Jesus.

Wet dream, any sex in the dream, I terminate you by the power of God in Jesus Christ.

Gynecological issues in my womb, Lord Jesus, flush them out, in the Name of Jesus.

Arrow of barrenness, fired against my life, go back to your owner, in Jesus' Name.

My good success, appear now, in the Name of Jesus.

Witchcraft powers attacking my womb, Holy Ghost Fire, shower down on them and swallow them up whole, in the Name of Jesus.

# Root Cause, Not Just Symptoms

Many times, a man ends up praying about the *symptoms* of a problem. He ends up asking for help with the *symptoms,* not a cure for the entire problem. Just as in medicine, sometimes we treat symptoms instead of the root cause. And sometimes we may never find out the spiritual root of something if we're only paying attention to the *symptoms*.

**It is kingly to search out a matter, (Proverbs 25:2).**

If we've never been taught, or if those needful things that should have been handed down from generation to generation have not been handed down, or if a rebellious young person just didn't listen when Grandma was talking, we may not learn of *root causes*. We especially may not learn the spiritual root causes of things. Being ignorant allows the devil to have his way against your life.

Perhaps your whole family was rebellious. Nobody was reading or sharing the Word. No one was teaching anybody, anything spiritual. No curse can come on a person unless they're out of step with God. When a man is in sin, he is in *covenant* with the devil.

At the open of this book that ignorant shopper was me. Ignorant, but happy. And in sin. So, if someone wanted to walk up on me with an **evil touch** except for the Mercy of God, they could have had their way.

When in a season of attack, because of your cry for Mercy, and because of God's heart toward us, He ***may not let the witch do anything to you***, but there is iniquity built into the sin that you had *fun* doing. Iniquity is a LAW. God may let the Blood of Jesus cry you out of natural laws, scientific and civil laws, but spiritually, there is iniquity for sins committed. Still, it is better to fall into the hands of God, than into the hands of a human because the human heart is wicked, deceitful and I will add here, JEALOUS.

David said to Gad, "I am in deep distress. Let us fall into the **hands** of the LORD, for his **mercy** is

great; but do not let me fall into human **hands**."
(2 Samuel 24:14)

The woman who assigned herself to oppose me in the spiritual department store was jealous, territorial, and possibly that man's s*pirit spouse of the p*hysical spirit spouse variety. She may have been evil, hateful, vengeful and insecure. I don't think it was a case of if you hurt my friend, I'm going to do XYZ to you because I didn't hurt him. No, I believe this is a matter of a woman chasing after a man. Like Shaggy I can say: *It wasn't me.*

WARNING: When you decide to get involved with anybody, you need to find out who that somebody is and who their friends are. Do they have spiritual protection, and if so, do they actively practice a religion? ***Who*** is their spiritual protection? If something goes awry, or if things don't work out as they should, who, spiritually speaking, is going to be mad at you? Are they serving a forgiving God? Are their *friends* forgiving people who also serve *Jehovah*?

Or are these evil, vengeful people who take matters into their own hands and invoke whatever evil, based on whatever altars they're serving at?

You'd better know. It would have been better for me had I known. It would definitely have been even better for me if I had not have been **sinning**, then the devil would have had nothing in me.

No, I'm not saying this visitor was powerful. My platform was higher, and she had no glory about her. Had I not been sinning she wouldn't have stepped to me at all, and she also would not have been able to touch me.

Because I have come to know, since leaving the **State of Ignorance,** that sometimes you can do absolutely nothing to a person, but they can still feel some kind of way toward you.

Or they could just have their sights set on something or someone that they want and will scorch Earth to get it. That person doesn't know what real love is. Love is voluntary. I learned that from God. God does not force us because that is captivity, not Love. To try to make a man be with you by blocking or attacking others is not Love.

It could be that in the accumulation of life and years that there's more than *one* evil altar coming at you, so maybe if you endure a fell swoop, it could be because that day, week or month you were not prayerful, *and* you were enticed to sin. So that one dark act was able to do more than they even thought because of the other altars.

Here, I'm talking about people who have evil altars, but they don't even know each other. Am I saying we roll up on a lot of witches in life? I'm saying, I have; I don't know about you.

I don't know they are witches because of the way they look. Their outfits aren't telling on them; they don't wear cone shaped hats or heavy makeup. They look just like regular folks. I'm just saying, because of what I know now and because I prayed, and the Lord has shown me, that's how I know, I've rolled up on a lot of them in my life. Rather, they have rolled up on me.

Witches roll up on people for their selfish and greedy reasons. *THAT* **you** don't roll up on people with selfish agendas is a sign that you are not a WITCH.

# Evil Laying on of Hands

There are evil people--, evil hirelings posing as pastors and there are false prophets. Pray very seriously about who you let touch you and even *more* seriously about who you let lay hands on you. Transference of *spirits* is possible. That's a worry, but **more** of a worry is that fake pastors and prophets may be doing the opposite of what you think; they can take virtue *from* you instead of imparting something to you.

Because of the evil laying on of hands a man may find it difficult to get successes in the natural. If a strange person or hand is touching you, pressing you down in the dream; pay attention and Pray up. If you refused a person in the natural, but at night there's a hand pressing you down in the dream, or some other astral projection or visitation, expect loss, weakness and difficulty in rising up, suspect foul powers. Cancel all these demonic dreams **immediately.**

**Prayer Points:**

Every evil hand that has brought trouble into my life, be neutralized by Fire, in the Name of Jesus.

Evil hand touching my destiny, to do me harm, catch Fire, in the Name of Jesus.

*Evil touch* that comes to steal, kill, destroy, exchange, or transfer problems into my life, wither, by FIRE. Touch of every evil hand, backfire!

Hands on my spouse, children or property in the dream, FIRE of God, paralyze those evil hands.

Anointing of TOUCH NOT. Come upon me now, in Jesus' Name.

Every evil hand oppressing my life day and night, wither by FIRE, and be destroyed by God, in Jesus' Name.

Anything that evil hands have stolen from me, LORD restore it back in Jesus' Name.

Lord, Arise and remove strange hands from the affairs of my life, in Jesus' Name.

# Evil Hands, *Wither*

Jeroboam's hand which he stretched out to seize or smite the man of God withered. May the Lord do the same for every ***evil touch*** that approaches you, in the spiritual or in the natural, in the Name of Jesus.

And it came to pass, when King Jeroboam heard the saying of the man of God who had cried against the altar in Bethel, that he put forth his hand from the altar, saying, "Lay hold on him!" And his hand, which he put forth against him, dried up, so that he could not pull it in back to him. (1 Kings 13:4)

**Prayer Points**:

Every evil touch and every evil load; back to senders, in the Name of Jesus.

I cancel every evil agenda of darkness for my life, in the Name of Jesus. I will NOT be renewing your contract or covenant, FOREVER.

Infirmity back to senders. I choose the LORD and He does not put the diseases of the Egyptians on me.

By Jesus Christ, I receive deliverance from the oppressor now, in the Name of Jesus.

Strongman sitting on my life. Sitting on my business, education, career, marriage, finances – go sit somewhere else. You are fired, you are bound, and you've got to go, in the Name of Jesus.

Every altar to disgrace me, catch your owner.

Altars speaking demotion to my life, receive demotion, destruction and desolation, today, in the Name of Jesus.

Every satanic priest ministering against me at any altar, no matter where it is, let your altar catch you now, in the Name of Jesus.

Evil hand, lose all power, and *wither*.
Evil hand, lose all strength, and **wither**.

Evil hand, lose your purpose, and **wither**.

Evil hand, **wither** by the power in the Blood of Jesus.

Evil hand, **wither** by the power in the Blood of Jesus. Amen.

Evil hand, forget my coordinates and lose my location, forever, and *wither*, in Jesus' Name.

Every power waiting for my downfall, lose sight of me and fall down yourself, in Jesus' Name.

Angels of the Living God, move against any power delaying my breakthrough, in Jesus' Name.

Every prison house jailing my destiny, open by Force, and let my destiny go free, in the Name of Jesus.

Every altar of stagnation assigned against me, my career, marriage, and children, backfire to sender(s) in the Name of Jesus.

Individual or coven evil HAND, *wither* by the power in the Blood of Jesus.

Every evil finger pointed at me, wither, in the Name of Jesus.

Every plan of the enemy against me--, FAIL!

Those discussing my life in order to hurt me, SCATTER!

He who wants to attack me with a magic arrow, ANGEL of God, retrieve the arrow from his hand and plant it inside of him, in the Name of Jesus.

Every evil plan concerning my life shall *wither* by the power in the Blood of Jesus.X7

Agenda of my enemies against my life, **wither**, in the Name of Jesus.

Large arrow of my enemies, come out of me, come out of my belly, come out of my back, come out of my hand, come out of my leg--,**WITHER** in the Name of Jesus. *(repeat several times)*.

Feet of my enemies, hear the Word of the LORD, *scatter* in the Name of Jesus.

Wicked altars assigned against my life, scatter and BURN, in the Name of Jesus.

Power source of my enemies, dry up, in the Name of Jesus.

Supporters of my enemies, *wither*, in the Name of Jesus.

Angry powers that pursued my ancestors you will not pursue me any longer; go to the pit, go to the Abyss, and never return, in the Name of Jesus.

Demonic army assigned against me, I set you into confusion. I release the war horses of the Lord against you, in the Name of Jesus.

Powers siphoning my blessings, return everything to me seven-fold, and *wither,* in the Name of Jesus.

Every evil gathering speaking failure into my life, *wither* by Fire, in the Name of Jesus.

Jeroboam powers of my father's house, what are you waiting for? *Wither* and DIE!! in the Name of Jesus.

Power of incantations ordered against me, *wither* in the Name of Jesus.

For every assignment of satanic hunters against my life, Divine Hunters, Fishers and Carpenters of God, capture my enemies and do not let them go again, in the Name of Jesus.

Eyes of darkness assigned to monitor me, *wither*, in the Name of Jesus.

Every power making covenants with the enemy to destroy me, DIE!!! In the Name of Jesus, we pray.

All unrepentant witchcraft, die the death of Jezebel, in the Name of Jesus.

Powers assigned to steal from me, *wither*, in the Name of Jesus.

# Deliver Me from Wicked Hands

In whose hands is a wicked scheme, And whose right hand is full of bribes, (Psalm 26:10)

Rescue me and deliver me out of the hand of aliens, whose mouth speaks deceit and whose right hand is a right hand of falsehood, (Psalm 144:11)

If left unchecked, evil hands can cage a person's destiny, family, marriage, relationships, finances, womb, and other vital areas of a person's life. They can put an evil mark on a person. They kill dreams. They snatch good things from the lives of good folks--, their entire lives because they don't know it's happening.

Deliver me, O Lord, from the evil man: preserve me from the violent man;Which imagine mischiefs in their heart; continually are they gathered together for

war. They have sharpened their tongues like a serpent; adders' poison is under their lips. Keep me, O Lord, from the hands of the wicked.
(Psalm 140:1-5)

## Prayers

I worship You, Lord, in the Name of JESUS. Lord, set me free from the bondage of sin, in the Name of JESUS.

Anything in me that will resist my prayess or keep them from being answered, be uprooted, in the Name of Jesus.

Earth, open and swallow now every hindrance to my answered prayers, in the Name of Jesus.

Demonic dream cops, assigned to arrest me, catch fire, lose your badge, lose your authority, lose your assignment against me, lose your power against me, in the Name of Jesus.

Every evil hand planning to work against me, lose your power, lose your connection to power, in the Name of Jesus.

Father, deliver my soul from the snare of the fowler, those lying in wait for me, in the Name of Jesus.

Evil hand of the wicked over my life, I will not bicker, if you like a snake do or do not slither, evil hand, evil woman, evil man, hand of evil against my life, wither by Fire, in the Name of Jesus.

Evil deposited in my life, by wicked hands, jump out by Fire, in the Name of Jesus.

Hand of the wicked manipulating my breakthrough wither away, slither away, in the Name of Jesus.

Father, by Your mighty outstretched Hand, save me from the plans of the wicked, in the Name of Jesus.

Father by Your power, let evil return to the preparer, in the Name of Jesus. (Psalm 140:11)

God arise, deliver me from the hand of wicked men, in the Name of Jesus. (Psalm 144:11)

Every effort to frustrate the angel of my answered prayer be cancelled by Fire, in the Name of Jesus.

I decode and nullify every new strategy of my enemies by the Blood of Jesus, in the Name of Jesus.

Father, thank You for setting me free from the hands of the wicked, in the Name of Jesus.

**Amen.**

# Strange Hands

Every evil hand behind the calamities you're facing there is probably a hand that has no business in your business. The evil hand that is working against your life, your family, your loved ones, must be stopped. If it will not repent and stop, it must be consumed by Fire, in the mighty Name of Jesus Christ.

Evil hands/*evil touch* are occultic in origin and driven by occultic powers. The intent is always to do harm, whereas the touch of God is to anoint, protect, and bless you.

You may know exactly who the evil hand is coming from. But if you don't, you will still need to pray to protect yourself, your family and to receive deliverance.

Don't look at people sideways; just pray. In no way am I suggesting that we should blame people for the disappointments of our lives --- we should look at ourselves first, then look at our family **history**. If we are prayerful, God will tell us everything we need to know by His Holy Spirit. Amen.

After you pray, be sure to be still and LISTEN.

A lot of individuals and families are suffering because of evil hands. An evil hand has blocked even the beautiful people from getting married or staying married. Some don't have children because of an *evil touch*. Poverty, which the government has decided to war against won't realize the success unless poverty is defeated *spiritually*, first. Evil hands haven't just stolen all the money out of the cookie jar, they have rendered *evil touch*, charmed by witchcraft to ruin the entire finances of their victims. They've broken the cookie jar, the piggy bank and maybe even the real bank if they have been unchecked.

The *evil touch* could have reached your degrees and educational certificates. If you are well educated but not enjoying a fruitful and abundant career, and life, suspect *evil touch*.

**Immediate Prayer Points:**

Evil hands behind poverty, insufficiency and lack, be cut off by the Fire of God, in the Name of Jesus.

Every evil hand, *evil touch* behind my change in circumstances to the negative, be consumed now by Holy Ghost Fire, in Jesus' Name.

Lord, thank You for Your weapons of war.

By Your Spirit cut off every evil meeting scheming against me now, in the Name of Jesus.

I cut off every evil hand working against my destiny, in the Name of Jesus.

*Evil touch* opposing my mind for business success, be cut off from your evil networks and power sources, in the Name of Jesus.

Evil hands, in my educational endeavors, be cut off from your evil sources, become confused and weak, in the Name of Jesus.

Lord, cancel every evil plan against my life. I return to the sender every evil plan, every evil charm, every wicked wish of the enemy, in Jesus' Name.

Mercy of God surround me completely, and send judgment on anyone seeking my destruction, in Jesus' Name.

Judgement Rain fall upon all those that wish me evil, in the Name of Jesus.

Everyone that wished me dead, let them reap the harvest of the evil that they wished for me, in the Name of Jesus.

Everyone that wishes me evil, let them live the hardness of the evil that they imagine for me, in the Name of Jesus Christ.

# Can't Touch This

God suffered no man to do them wrong; yea, he reproved kings for thy sakes; Saying, Touch not mine anointed, and do my prophets no harm.
(Psalm 105:14-15)

Dreams of *visitations* from strangers who are trying to touch you are bad. If you see such a stranger in a dream, it is out to harm you. Do not touch them. Do not hug them. Do not let them touch you. Do not give them your hand. Even if it looks like someone you know because the devil often uses masquerades.

Do not let a masqueraded "pastor," for example, pray for you or lay hands on you in the dream.

We have to pray against **evil touch**. The Lord will contend with those that contend with you and God will save your children, (Jeremiah 17:9).

The ***evil touch*** is a touch of sickness, affliction, of poverty, of death, a touch of stagnation and delay. Its purpose is to bring sorrow and break up your relationships, chiefly your marriage.

Lord, in the Name of Jesus deliver me from all **evil touch**.

Touch of sexual of the sexual organs may lead to diseases, and disorders such as incontinence. Bed wetting and urinary leaks during the day is incontinence, and it is DEFILEMENT. Do you want to get on a prescription medicine to stop incontinence, or would you like to handle it at the **root** of the problem, in the Spirit and be done with it?

**Prayer Points:**

LORD, destroy the charm of the evil ones that approach me in my dreams or in bold daylight *visitations* to touch me, or to touch my life. My life is a gift from God, it is none of their business. I reject them Lord, and all of their business. Cancel all their wickedness against me, in Jesus' Name. Send them to the feet of Jesus for ministry, but if they are reprobate, deal with them according to Your Word.

LORD, protect me and protect your investment in me. Lord, I have sinned and fallen short of the Glory of God; I need Your Mercy.

Lord, forgive my sins, my evil thoughts, plans, and my transgressions and forgive. LORD JESUS, forgive the iniquity of my sin.

Forgive ancestral sin back to or before Adam & Eve. Restore my glory, Lord, and my *essence* in Jesus' Name.

Lord, I break evil covenants, curses, ancestral and ancient altars. I bind and fire every demon assigned to enforce torment and any curse against me, in the Name of Jesus.

Jesus, my Great Intercessor, pray for me; speak for me. Blood of Jesus answer for me. I cry, *Mercy. Mercy, Mercy*, in the Name of Jesus.

Lord, where I have attracted **evil touch**, or defiled myself or sinned to not be able to ward off **evil touch**, Lord, forgive me. Lord, deliver me from all evil, especially **evil touch** by evil and strange hands, for thine is the Kingdom, the power and the glory, forever. Amen.

Spirit of Grace and prayer come upon me in this ***Season of Warfare***, in the Name of Jesus.

Every adversary fighting me in the dream, I command you to be destroyed and disconnected from the power that you worship, be disconnected from your coven, and disconnected from the altar at which you serve. I break your network, in the Name of Jesus.

Any power that has sworn that I will not live to see the end of this year, you die, in the Name of Jesus. Whatever evil you have planned for me, you have it and leave my premises, leave my life, **leave the realm where I *dwell*, in the Name of Jesus.**

Lord Jesus, every entity that walks or stalks me or my family at night, I bind them, in the Name of Jesus. Lord put a Fire of protection around me, my family, my spouse, my children, my house and everything under my stewardship, in the Name of Jesus. Every evil attempt against my family, fail woefully by the Blood of Jesus, in the Name of Jesus.

I seal every access point to me, my family my home and everything under my stewardship by the Blood of Jesus, in the Name of Jesus.

Evil hands, ***wither*** in the Name of Jesus.

Evil touch be nullified, in the Name of Jesus.

Evil plans against me, backfire, in the Name of Jesus.

Every evil power planning to use me or my family as sacrifice, we are not your candidates. Jesus, the Mighty Warrior, the King of Glory, Jehovah Sabaoth, answer for me and contend with those that contend with me, in the Name of Jesus.

Every evil hand that has introduced the *spirit of lust* to my spouse or children, I bind and break the *spirit of lust* off them, and I command the owners of those evil hands to die by Fire, die by Fire, die by Fire, in the Name of Jesus.

Every evil hand that has come to introduce sickness, disease, poverty, lack, insufficiency, destitution, barrenness, cursed hands, cursed feet, cursed leg, cursed mind, any curse of any body part or organ you are exiled from my presence and my life by the King of Glory; Lord Jesus rebuke them and send them to where You have prepared a place for them.

Every unrepentant, evil human agent, I commend you to the Lord Jesus Christ to be dealt with as the Lord Jesus sees fit.

Powers of darkness, scatter. You are not invited here, you are not welcomed here, and you have no cause to be here as well as no access; scatter and die. Go to the Abyss for early torment and never return to me, my family, my life or touch any of us or anything over which I have stewardship again, in Jesus' Name.

Strange and estranged women who desire my husband, I decree that the exact evil you planned for me shall come upon you suddenly and mightily, in the Name of Jesus.

Every *evil touch* meant to lead to any dread disease, any terminal disease, disorder or syndrome I cancel your touch RIGHT NOW. May the Lord deal with the sender according to that sender's heart, in the Name of Jesus.

Cancer: I cancel you out of my body and life, in the Name of Jesus.

Diabetes: I cancel you out of my body and life, in the Name of Jesus.

Heart Disease: I cancel you out of my body and life now, in the Name of Jesus.

Any blood, breathing, respiratory, muscular or joint disorder as a result of ***evil touch***, I do not receive it.

I cancel every evil affect over my body and life.

I deflect your hands with my Shield of Faith, and I cause it to return back to you--, Back to Sender.

Every beauty curse and spell sent against me, I cancel you out of my body and life. Every beauty exchange, I demand you change back and restore my beauty and glory, in the Name of Jesus.

Obesity, I cancel you out of my body and life now, in the Name of Jesus – BACK TO SENDER. *You be a Clump. I'm not a Clump, I'm a Child of God.*

I declare that my metabolism works as God intended from my inception and birth – or even more efficiently.

My joints and muscles are strong so I can move and exercise easily, in the natural.

My movement, health, and life Glorifies the Father, in Jesus' Name.

I decree, I shall not die; I shake off every affliction intended for me and return it back to sender, in the Name of Jesus.

I take back all my eggs from every evil hand.

My womb, be made whole, well, fertile, strong: I shall no longer be called barren, in the Name of Jesus.

Lord, thank You for the Wisdom to handle the knowledge that You've given me since leaving the **State of Ignorance**, in the Name of Jesus.

Thank You, Lord for answering these prayers, we count it as done, in the matchless Name of Jesus.

Lord, thank You that everything about my mind, my soul, my body, my spirit is healed, by the stripes of Jesus.

I renounce and break all evil contracts, all generational curses, covenants and bondages.

I repent of all sin, in the Name of Jesus.

Lord, forgive me, cleanse me with the Blood of Jesus. Renew a right *Spirit* in me.

Father, by Holy Ghost Fire, break me free from all contracts, covenants, deal, soul ties, evil altars, and curses, by the Blood of Jesus, in the Name of Jesus.

I bind every demon assigned to hurt me, torment or enforce any curse against me or my body, my mind, my soul, my spirit, my life, my family, in the Name of Jesus.

Touch me Lord and keep all ***evil touches*** away from me, in the Name of Jesus.

I bear in my body the marks of the Lord Jesus Christ, and I abide under the wings of the Almighty God.

Satan. Do not touch me, do not touch any part of me, not my soul, not my spirit, not my body, in the Name of Jesus. **Hands off**, in the Name of Jesus. Amen.

# Prayerbooks by this author

While most books by this author have prayer points either throughout the book or at the end, there are some books that are only prayers. You just open up the book and pray. They are listed below:

**Prayers Against Barrenness:** *For Success in Business and Life*

**Fruit of the Womb:** *Prayers Against Barrenness*

**Beauty Curses,** *Warfare Prayers Against*
https://a.co/d/5Xlc20M

**Courts of Marriage: Prayers for Marriage in the Courts of Heaven** *(prayerbook)* https://a.co/d/cNAdgAq

**Courtroom Warfare @ Midnight** *(prayerbook)*
https://a.co/d/5fc7Qdp

**Demonic Cobwebs** *(prayerbook)* https://a.co/d/fp9Oa2H

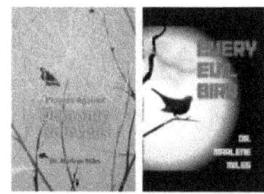

Every Evil Bird https://a.co/d/hF1kh1O

Gates of Thanksgiving

Spirits of Death, Hell & the Grave, Pass Over Me and My House

Throne of Grace: Courtroom Prayer

Warfare Prayer Against Poverty
https://a.co/d/bZ611Yu

# Other books by this author

AK: The Adventures of the Agape Kid

Already Married in the Spirit: *Why You May Not Be Married in the Natural*

AMONG SOME THIEVES

Ancestral Powers

Anti-Marriage, *The Spirit of*

Backstabbers https://a.co/d/gi8iBxf

Barrenness, *Prayers Against*
https://a.co/d/feUltIs

Battlefield of Marriage, *The*

Beware of the Dog: Prayers Against Dogs in the Dream.

Bless Your Food: *Let the Dining Table be Undefiled*

Blindsided: *Has the Old Man Bewitched You?*
https://a.co/d/5O2fLLR

Break Free from Collective Captivity

Broken Spirits & Dry Bones

Casting Down Imaginations

Churchzilla, The Wanna-Be, Supposed-to-be Bride of Christ

Demonic Cobwebs (prayerbook)

Demonic Time Bombs

Demons Hate Questions

Devil Loves Trauma, *The*

Devil Weapons: Unforgiveness, Bitterness,...

The Devourers: Thieves of Darkness 2

Do Not Swear by the Moon

Don't Refuse Me, Lord (4 book series)
https://a.co/d/idP34LG

Dream Defilement

The Emptiers: *Thieves of Darkness, 1*
https://a.co/d/5I4n5mc

Evil Touch

Failed Assignment

Fantasy Spirit Spouse https://a.co/d/hW7oYbX

FAT Demons (The): *Breaking Demonic Curses*
https://a.co/d/4kP8wV1

The Fold (5-book series)

- The Fold (Book 1)
- Name Your Seed (Book 2)
- The Poor Attitudes of Money (3)
- Do Not Orphan Your Seed (4)
- For the Sake of the Gospel (5)
- My Sowing Journal

Gang Ups: Touch Not God's Anointed

Getting Rid of Evil Spiritual Food

https://a.co/d/i2L3WYQ

got HEALING? Verses for Life

got LOVE? Verses for Life

got HOPE? Verses for Life

got money? https://a.co/d/g2av41N

How to Dental Assist

How to Dental Assist2: Be Productive, Not Wasteful

How to STOP Being a Blind Witch or Warlock

I Take It Back

Legacy

Let Me Have A Dollar's Worth
https://a.co/d/h8F8XgE

Level the Playing Field

Living for the NOW of God

Lose My Location https://a.co/d/crD6mV9

Love Breaks Your Heart

Made Perfect In Love

Man Safari, *The*

Marriage Ed. Rules of Engagement & Marriage

Made Perfect in Love

Money Hunters: Beware of Those

Money on the Altar https://a.co/d/4EqJ2Nr

Mulberry Tree, *The* https://a.co/d/9nR9rRb

Motherboard (The) - *Soul Prosperity Series*

Name Your Seed

Occupy: *Until I Return*

Plantation Souls

Players Gonna Play

Power Money: Nine Times the Tithe
https://a.co/d/gRt41gy

The Power of Wealth *(forthcoming)*

Powers Above

The Robe, Part 1, The Lessons of Joseph

The Robe, Part II, The Lessons of Joseph

Seasons of Grief

Seasons of Waiting

Seasons of War  https://a.co/d/0RBkyh8

Second Marriage, Third~~, *Any Marriage*

https://a.co/d/6m6GN4N

Sift You Like Wheat

Six Men Short: What Has Happened to all the Men?

Soul Prosperity soul prosperity series 3

https://a.co/d/5p8YvCN

Souls Captivity soul prosperity series 2

The Spirit of Anti-Marriage

The Spirit of Poverty

StarStruck

SUNBLOCK

The Swallowers: *Thieves of Darkness*, 3

Take It Back

This Is NOT That: How to Keep Demons from Coming at You

Time Is of the Essence

Too Many Wives: *Why You Have Lady Problems*

Tormenting Spirits https://a.co/d/dAogEJf

Toxic Souls

Triangular Power *(series)*

- Powers Above
- SUNBLOCK
- Do Not Swear by the Moon
- STARSTRUCK

Unbreak My Heart: *Don't Let Me Die*

Uncontested Doom

Unguarded Hours, *The*

Unseen Life, *The* (forthcoming)

Upgrade: How to Get Out of Survival Mode

- Toxic Souls (Book 2 of series)
- Legacy (Book 3 of series)

The Wasters: *Thieves of Darkness*, Bk 2
https://a.co/d/bUvI9Jo

What Have You to Declare? What Do You Have With You from Where You've Been?

When I Was A Child, *I Prayed As a Child*

When the Devourer is Rebuked

https://a.co/d/1HVv8oq

**The Wilderness Romance** *(series)* This series is about conducting a Godly relationship and marriage with someone who is a Wilderness person. It is about how to recognize it and navigate through it.

These books are about how not to get caught up in such.

- *The Social Wilderness*
- *The Sexual Wilderness*
- *The Spiritual Wilderness*

## Other Series

**The Fold (a series on Godly finances)**
https://a.co/d/4hz3unj

**Soul Prosperity Series** https://a.co/d/bz2M42q

## Spirit Spouse books

https://a.co/d/9VehDSo

https://a.co/d/97sKOwm

 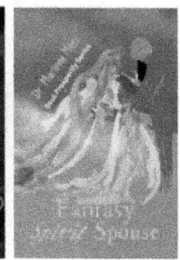

**Battlefield of Marriage, The**

https://a.co/d/eUDzizO

**Players Gonna Play**

https://a.co/d/2hzGw3N

## Matters of the Heart

Made Perfect in Love https://a.co/d/7OMQW3O

Love Breaks Your Heart https://a.co/d/4KvuQLZ

Unbreak My Heart https://a.co/d/84ceZ6M

Broken Spirits & Dry Bones https://a.co/d/e6iedNP

## Thieves of Darkness series

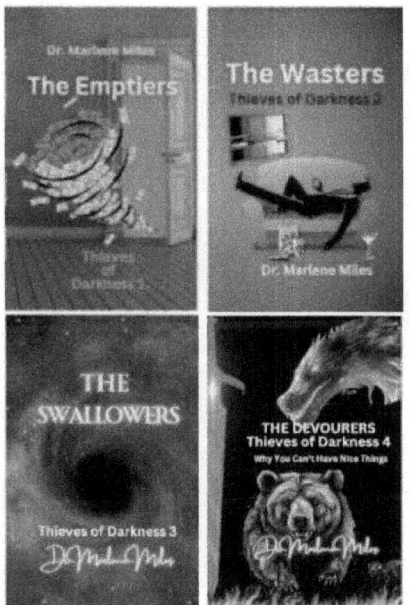

The Emptiers https://a.co/d/heio0dO

The Wasters https://a.co/d/5TG1iNQ

The Swallowers https://a.co/d/1jWhM6G

**The Devourers: Why We Can't Have Nice Things**
https://a.co/d/87Tejbf

**Triangular Powers** https://a.co/d/aUCjAWC

**Upgrade** (series) *How to Get Out of Survival Mode*
https://a.co/d/aTERhXO

www.ingramcontent.com/pod-product-compliance
Lightning Source LLC
Chambersburg PA
CBHW070203100426
42743CB00013B/3031